the story of the U.S.A.

Book 1
Explorers and Settlers

by Franklin Escher, Jr.

Educators Publishing Service
Cambridge and Toronto

Educators Publishing Service
800.225.5750
www.epsbooks.com

Printed in U.S.A.
ISBN 0-8388-1631-2
978-0-8388-1631-8

17 18 19 20 PPG 16

Table of Contents

For the Student

Welcome to the world of American history. You are going to read about our country's past. History is filled with exciting stories and interesting people. This book will tell you about some of them. It can also help you practice ways to read and study that you can use in all your classes, not just in history class.

Before you start working in this book, you will need to know how it is put together. Each chapter is arranged into parts that take you along one step at a time. If you follow the directions, you will be able to read and learn the material without any trouble.

To begin with, there are pictures and sometimes maps at the start of each chapter. By studying them, you will get an idea of what you are going to be reading about.

Next, there are a few vocabulary words. This vocabulary section gives meanings and pronunciations for some words that will appear in the chapter. The letters in CAPITALS are parts of the word which are accented, or said the loudest:

example = eg-ZAM-pul

Turn next to the chapter story. At the beginning are two or three questions, just beneath the title. These give you some hints about the main ideas and help you start thinking *before* you read. Keep these questions in mind, and look for the answers as you read the chapter.

Some words in the chapter story are printed in heavy black type called **boldface**. These are the words from the vocabulary page. Some other words and names are printed in *italics*. That is a signal to look at the right-hand column of the page if you need help in pronouncing them.

One more thing to look for is a black dot ●. Most chapters are divided into sections, with a dot to show that a main section has come to an end. That should be your signal to stop and think back over the paragraphs in that section. Try to tell yourself the main ideas that were discussed. Ask yourself WHAT happened, WHO did it, and WHY. A quick review like this helps you take the facts and ideas from a book and put them into your own words. That is the best way of all to study.

At the end of each chapter you will find exercises to do. Don't think of these as a test. They are designed to help you review the most important facts and ideas in the chapter. As you work along through the book, think carefully about what you are reading. It will help you to do the exercises without having to look back at the chapter.

Exercise A always deals with the main ideas. Ideas are even more important than facts. If you know the main ideas of a story, you understand its meaning. For example, it is just as important to know *why* Columbus came to America as it is to know *when* he came (1492).

Exercise C or D is a vocabulary review. This exercise should be easy. It is designed to help you strengthen and build your vocabulary by giving you extra practice with the words from the first page of the chapter. You will see some of those words again and again in later parts of the book. The last exercise in each chapter is called "Think About and Discuss in Class." Here, you and your classmates can begin to relate the past to the present and to your own lives. You can look for the lessons that history can teach us. Why do wars start? Why do people starve? How can the world be made a happier place to live in?

History teaches us lessons, and it is fun to read. You'll enjoy the stories of the first explorers and settlers of America. Some of them were heroes, some villains, and some were a little of both. Pick out your favorites and talk about them in class.

As you turn these pages, you will find yourself reading faster and faster. Keep it up! Within a short time, you will be moving easily through this book. It will help make you a better reader and a better student.

We can learn about the first Americans by studying the things they made. Shown here are spear and arrow points, a pot, a bone needle, a stone ax head, and a stone for grinding corn.

After living as hunters for many centuries, Native Americans began to grow crops. Many of them became farmers.

Getting Ready for Chapter One

1

Here are six vocabulary words that are used in the story of the first Americans. Study these definitions so you will know what each word means when you see it in your reading.

strait   (STRAYT)   A narrow channel of water that connects two oceans or seas.

ancestors   (AN-ses-turz)   Members of our family who lived long ago, before our time.

ancient   (AYN-chent)   Very old. Belonging to times long ago.

artifacts   (AR-tuh-fakts)   Things made by humans long ago.

centuries   (SEN-chur-eez)   Hundreds of years. One century is a hundred years long.

native   (NAY-tiv)   Belonging to a certain country or place because one was born there.

The first people to reach America came from Asia. They crossed over to Alaska and slowly moved south. Finally, there were Native American settlements all the way down to the tip of South America.

At first, the ancient Americans lived by hunting.

The First Americans

The first people to live in America did not come by boat.
How do you think they got here?
How long ago did they reach this land?

Long ago there were no people living in this land—no people at all. There were no cities, streets, and buildings. There was no United States. The eastern forests were so thick that squirrels could jump from tree to tree without touching the ground for hundreds of miles. To the west lay deserts, plains, and mountains. Wild animals were the only living things.

About forty thousand years ago, hunters from *Asia* traveled across frozen land and ice into Alaska. We think they were the first Americans. They crossed at the *Bering* Strait, a strip of ocean where Asia and Alaska almost touch. Scientists believe that in those days, there was no water in the **strait**.

AY-zhuh

BEER-ing

The first Americans moved from place to place hunting for food. From Alaska, they and the people who lived after them pushed south into the empty wilderness. Finally, their settlements reached all the way to the tip of South America.

These first Americans formed many different nations. They were the **ancestors** of today's **Native** Americans. Native Americans are also known as American Indians. •

How do we know that these things happened? No written proof has been found because no one in those days knew how to read or write. But the first Americans left their story in stones and bones for us to read.

Bones of **ancient** animals have been found in Alaska. Spear points found in these bones show that the animals were killed by human beings. Scientists can measure the age of the bones. The measurements prove that those animals and the hunters who killed them lived more than twenty thousand years ago. Near Midland, Texas, the bones of what was once a young woman were found. Tests show that she died twelve thousand years ago.

Animals' bones found in Mexico in 1959 are believed to be thirty thousand years old. There are beautiful pictures of cats and snakes carved on the bones. These *decorations* were made by human beings.

dek-or-AY-shunz

Objects made by human hands are called **artifacts**. Spearheads are artifacts. So are knives and stone hatchets and cooking pots. Scientists and historians look for ancient artifacts everywhere on earth. Artifacts tell us about our past. •

As **centuries** went by, the first Americans learned ways to make their living safer and easier. They invented the bow and arrow. This *weapon* made them very powerful against most animals.

WEP-un

The Native Americans made animal furs into clothes. They sewed the furs with needles made from slivers of bone. Cups, spoons, saucers, baskets, and other artifacts were carved and woven.

The early Americans began to raise corn and other crops for food. Some of them stopped being hunters and became farmers. They built homes near each other and worked together. In this way, towns and cities came into being. Then, rules and laws had to be made. Chiefs and rulers told the people what to do. •

We cannot think of Native Americans as one people who were all alike. The tribes spoke different *languages* and lived in different ways. Some were warlike, while others were peaceful. Some lived in tents, while others lived in stone buildings. There were fishermen, farmers, hunters, *priests*, and weavers.

LAN-gwij-iz

PREESTS
YOOR-up

The Native Americans were here long before people from *Europe* and Africa arrived. The next chapter will tell more about the life of these ancient Americans.

Answer these to review the main ideas.

A.

1. Who were the first Americans? _____

_____

   Where do we think they came from? _____

_____

   How long ago did they come? _____

_____

   How far south did the first Americans finally go? _____

_____

2. **How can we learn about what happened in the past?** _____

_____

_____

3. Name three things the Native Americans did that made their way of

   living better. _____

_____

_____

_____

Circle True or False.

T F 1. There have always been people living in America.

T F 2. The first Americans came from Africa.

T F 3. Hunters wandered into Alaska about forty thousand years ago.

T F 4. None of the early Americans got to South America.

T F 5. Something made by a human being is an artifact.

T F 6. All Native Americans spoke the same language and lived in the same way.

T F 7. The first Americans could read and write.

B.

Circle the right answer to finish each sentence.

C.

1. Asia and Alaska almost touch each other at

   a. Mexico   b. the Bering Strait   c. Texas

2. The first Americans were

   a. farmers   b. soldiers   c. hunters

3. They became more powerful hunters when they invented the

   a. spear   b. bow and arrow   c. hatchet

4. Scientists can tell how long ago an animal lived by testing its

   a. bones   b. tracks   c. fur

5. Native Americans learned to sew with needles made of

   a. metal   b. stone   c. bone

6. The ancient Americans built homes near each other and worked together after they learned to

   a. grow crops   b. hunt   c. make clothes

Choose one of these words to fit each sentence below.

D.

strait   ancestors   ancient

artifacts   native   century

1. Things made by people who lived long ago are called

_____ .

5

2. A channel of water that connected the Atlantic Ocean with the Pacific Ocean could be called a _____ .

3. Mary and Joe were born in Chicago and are _____ to that city.

4. There are one hundred years in a _____ .

5. Something very old is called _____ .

6. Our relatives who lived long ago are our _____ .

Think about and discuss in class.

E.

Chapter One tells us about the first Americans, who lived thousands of years ago. Have you ever counted to a thousand? By the time you got to five hundred, you were probably sorry you ever started! Try counting now. One, two, three . . . four, five, six, and so on. Imagine that every time you count a number, a whole year goes by. This may give you a feeling of how long a thousand years really is!

Are stones artifacts? Explain your answer._____

_____

Would you expect to find artifacts on the moon, or on Mars? Why or

why not? _____

_____

_____

The Pueblo people raised corn, beans, and squash.

Getting Ready for Chapter Two

2

Here are six vocabulary words that are used in the story of how Native Americans lived. Study these definitions so you will know what each word means when you see it in your reading.

continent	(KON-tuh-nent) A huge piece of land. The earth's seven continents are: North America, South America, Europe, Asia, Africa, Australia, and Antarctica.
council	(KOUN-sul) A group of people who meet together to make laws or rules.
Latin America	(LAT-un) A name for the lands south of the United States where most people now speak Spanish or Portuguese, but where several other older languages are still spoken.
civilization	(siv-uh-luh-ZAY-shun) An advanced way of living. Civilized people usually have laws and a government and know something about science. "Native American civilization" means their way of life.
sacrifice	(SAK-ruh-fys) Something a person gives up, or gives to a god.
mathematics	(math-uh-MAT-iks) The science that studies numbers and measurements.

The Iroquois, who lived in New York State, were famous fighters. The Maya of Mexico played a game like basketball.

In the southwestern part of the United States, the Pueblo people built high-rise homes. They used ladders to go from one floor to another.

How the Native Americans Lived

This chapter tells about Native American life.
Try to remember some of the things each group did.
Which ones lived in apartment houses?
Which ones built bridges and roads?

Before white people came to America from Europe, the Native Americans were spread out over the **continents** of North and South America. There were many groups, more than we can tell about here.

Eskimos lived in Alaska, Canada, and Greenland. They were the last group of people to come over from Asia. The Eskimos hunted for deer on land and for seals, whales, and fish in the water. They dressed warmly in animal furs and skins. Some of them lived in houses made of snow.

The *Iroquois* lived farther south, in land that is now New York State. There were five tribes of Iroquois, bound together in peace and war. The Iroquois were famous for their strength and courage.

IHR-uh-kwoy

Hunting, farming, and making war kept the Iroquois busy. They lived in "long houses" built of bark and poles. Each long house held several families, and a group of long houses made up a village. Each village was surrounded by walls for *protection*.

pruh-TEK-shun

Women were highly thought of among the Iroquois. Women helped choose the chiefs. They spoke out in the **council** meetings to help make rules for the tribes.

In the southwest part of our land lived the *Pueblo* people. The Pueblos were peaceful farmers who raised corn, beans, and squash. Cotton was also grown and made into clothes and blankets.

PWEB-low

The Pueblos built the first high-rise apartment houses in America. Some were eight stories high. Instead of *elevators*, they used ladders to get from floor to floor. When enemies came, the Pueblos raced up high in the buildings, pulling the ladders up after them. From there, they could fight back or try to make an escape. •

EL-uh-vay-turz

To the south in **Latin America**, several groups of early Americans built great **civilizations**. This means that they learned to work together and to make laws. It means that they had buildings, cities, roads, bridges, and farms. They carved golden *statues*, painted colorful pictures, and wore beautiful clothes.

STACH-ooz

Religion was very important to them. When the Aztecs, who lived in Mexico, thought their gods were angry, they offered them gifts. The best gift, they believed, was human lives. In their temples, the priests carved out the hearts of young men and offered them to the gods as a **sacrifice**. Young women were thrown off the tops of the temples. While these things happened, thousands of people chanted and sang and beat drums to please the gods.

ree-LIJ-un

The Maya, who also lived in Mexico, studied the sky. From the way the sun and stars moved every year, they learned to tell time and to use a *calendar*. They understood **mathematics** and invented a way to write. Their favorite sport was a game much like our own basketball.

KAL-un-dur

In South America the most important *region* was *Peru*. This was the land of the Incas, who ruled from high in the mountains. The Incas had a wonderful set of roads and bridges to connect their cities and towns. Some bridges were so high in the air that it was scary to look down. *Messengers* ran along the roads carrying orders from the king to all parts of the Inca land. •

REE-jun   puh-ROO

MES-un-jurz

Native American nations differed from each other in their languages and customs. Yet they were alike in certain ways. The ancient Americans *respected* nature — the sun, the wind, trees, and mountains. And they believed in sharing things, not owning them. The land belonged to everybody, not to any one person or persons.

ree-SPEKT-id

Native Americans were alike in another way, too. If you look at pictures of their life long ago, you will see no carts or wagons. They did not use wheels, except in toys. Today wheels carry people and goods from place to place. Wheels are needed to run machines. But even without wheels, the early Americans built great civilizations.

Answer these to review the main ideas.

A.

1. Which Native Americans lived the farthest north? _____

_____

2. What were the Iroquois famous for? _____

_____

3. What kind of homes did the Pueblos build? _____

_____

What crops did they grow? _____

_____

4. Which ancient Americans lived in Latin America? _____

_____

How did the Maya learn to tell time and to use a calendar? _____

_____

Where did the Incas live?_____

_____

_____

_____

_____

5. In what ways were the different groups of Native Americans alike?

   a. _____

   b. _____

   c. _____

Circle True or False.

T   F   1. The Eskimos grew corn and squash.

T   F   2. The Pueblo people were a warlike tribe.

T   F   3. The ancient Americans in Latin America built great civilizations.

T   F   4. Native Americans respected nature.

T   F   5. Native Americans thought it was wrong to share things.

Circle the right answer to finish each sentence.

1. The Eskimos wore clothes made from

   a. fur   b. cotton   c. bark

2. Women took part in the council meetings of the

   a. Incas   b. Iroquois   c. Pueblos

3. The Pueblo people went from floor to floor in their houses by using

   a. ladders   b. elevators   c. ropes

4. The Aztecs in Mexico thought that the best gift for their gods was

   a. food   b. gold   c. human lives

5. The ancient Americans never made use of

   a. arrows   b. wheels   c. spears

6. Roads and bridges were built by the

   a. Pueblos   b. Iroquois   c. Incas

B.

C.

11

Choose one of these words to fit each sentence below.

D.

    continent   Latin America   sacrifice

    council   civilization   mathematics

1. When people know how to use numbers and measurements, we say that they know _____ .

2. People who get together to make the rules for their group are a _____.

3. The American lands where most people now speak Spanish or Portuguese are known as _____.

4. The _____s are the world's largest pieces of land.

5. When human beings were killed as gifts to the gods, they were used as _____s.

6. People have a _____ if they work together and have cities and laws and science and art.

Think about and discuss in class.

E.

What would our lives be like today if we had no wheels? What wouldn't we be able to do? _____

_____

_____

_____

_____

How could we visit someone fifty miles away without using wheels? ___

_____

Suppose you could go back in time and join a group of Native Americans anywhere in North or South America. Which group would you choose? _____

Why? _____

_____

_____

When Columbus reached some islands near the coast of America, it was a turning point in history. But it was not good news for Native Americans.

Getting Ready for Chapter Three

3

Here are four vocabulary words that are used in the story of Columbus. Study these definitions so you will know what each word means when you see it in your reading.

voyage   (VOY-ij)   A trip made on a ship.

colony   (KOL-uh-nee)   A group of people who settle in a new land. The settlement that they make.

precious   (PRESH-us)   Worth a great deal, very valuable.

stubborn   (STUB-urn)   Not willing to give up. Hard to change.

Columbus found the New World, but it was named after a different Italian explorer called Americus Vespucius.

Columbus's sailors were afraid they might fall off the edge of the world. Some thought they might be eaten by sea monsters.

Columbus believed he could get to Asia by sailing west. The distance did not seem far. But his maps were wrong. No one knew that the Atlantic Ocean did not run all the way to Asia. No one knew that two whole continents were in the way.

Columbus Comes to America

Did you know that Columbus landed on an island,
and not on the shore of America itself?

What was Columbus really looking for?
Did he find it?

On October 12, 1492, Native Americans living on an island near Florida stared out to sea in wonder. Three ships with sails and colorful flags appeared off the shore. The ships' cannons boomed a loud *signal*. Men with bearded white faces climbed down into small boats and rowed to the beach. When they reached shore, the men got down on their knees and prayed. They gave thanks for their safe **voyage** to that unknown land.

SIG-nul

As the frightened islanders continued to watch, the leader of these strange-looking visitors stepped forward. He wore a bright red cape. Raising his sword, the leader said, "I take this island in the name of the King and Queen."

The leader was *Christopher Columbus*. He had been hired by the king and queen of Spain. Columbus had started out from the continent of Europe, thousands of miles away. He and his men had sailed across the Atlantic Ocean and found America.

KRIS-tuh-fur
kuh-LUM-bus

This event was a great moment in history — but not for the Native Americans. After the voyage of Columbus, Europeans began to settle in North America and South America. They started many **colonies**. Slowly but surely, the new settlers took the land away from the people who already lived there.

Columbus arrived in America by accident. He really was looking for the continent of Asia. **Precious** jewels and spices had been discovered on the Asian continent. The way to go there from Europe — and to get rich — was to travel east. Ships from Europe used to sail all the way around Africa to reach eastern Asia.

Columbus believed that there was a quicker way to reach Asia. His idea was to sail WEST from Europe. Maps of his time showed only one ocean in the world. Europe was on the eastern side, and Asia was on the west. The distance across this ocean did not seem far. But the maps were wrong. They did not show the Americas or the wide *Pacific* Ocean.

puh-SIF-ik

Columbus was strong and **stubborn**. When he made up his mind to do something, he stuck with it. His men obeyed him, even though they were afraid. Many of them believed that the earth was flat. If a ship sailed too far, it would fall off the edge of the world. The sailors also thought that terrible monsters swam in the ocean. No one had ever been out so far from land.

When Columbus finally landed in America, he thought he was in Asia. He did not know that Asia was still thousands of miles away. To his dying day, Columbus believed that he had landed in Asia, near China and India. He called the islands he found "the Indies," and he called the people living there "Indians."

After reaching America, Columbus went on a sightseeing *tour*. He visited Cuba and other islands nearby. About the Native Americans, he had this to say: "I do not believe there is a better people in the world. They love their neighbors as themselves."

TOOR

Columbus looked for palaces, cities, and gold mines. Asia had such riches. But there was no *wealth* in the part of America Columbus visited. The people that he saw lived and dressed very simply.

WELTH

When Columbus returned to Spain he was treated like a hero. The King and Queen listened eagerly to him. He promised to bring them gold and jewels next time. But he never did.

Columbus made three more trips to America. But he could not find anything of *value*. The king and queen of Spain grew angry with him. Columbus died a lonely and unhappy man.

VAL-yoo

Even the New World that Columbus found was named for someone else. Columbus was an Italian. A different Italian explorer had America named after himself. His first name was *Americus*. This man boasted about his travels and became famous. His name appeared in books and on maps. So the two new continents were called the Americas, instead of being named for Columbus.

uh-MAIR-uh-kus

Answer these to review the main ideas.

A.

1. When did Columbus come to America? _____

_____

Who paid for his trip? _____

_____

2. Was Columbus looking for America? _____

_____

What place was he looking for? _____

_____

What did he think was the best way to get there?_____

_____

3. What did Columbus promise to bring the king and queen of Spain?

_____

_____

Was he able to keep this promise? _____

B. Circle True or False.

T F 1. The arrival of Columbus in America was a great moment in history for the Native Americans.

T F 2. Maps used in the time of Columbus were wrong.

T F 3. The king and queen of Spain became angry at Columbus.

T F 4. An Italian explorer named Americus said that the New World should be named for Columbus.

T F 5. Columbus thought he had found Asia.

T F 6. Columbus landed on an island near Florida.

C. Circle the right answer to finish each sentence.

1. Columbus reached America in

   a. 1620   b. 1553   c. 1492

2. Christopher Columbus was

   a. Italian   b. Spanish   c. Native American

3. Columbus was hired by the king and queen of

   a. Italy   b. Spain   c. Asia

4. What Columbus really hoped to find was

   a. America   b. Africa   c. Asia

5. Europeans went to Asia to get

   a. jewels and spices   b. oil   c. slaves

6. Most people got to Asia by sailing

   a. east   b. north   c. west

7. Columbus thought he could get to Asia by sailing

   a. east   b. north   c. west

Choose one of these words to fit each sentence below.

precious   stubborn   voyage   colony

1. When a country makes a settlement in a strange land, it has started

   a _____ .

2. In the days of sailing ships, a _____ across the ocean took a long time.

3. Something that has great value is _____ .

4. A man or woman whose mind is hard to change is a _____ person.

Think about and discuss in class.

Columbus arriving in America is sometimes compared with men landing on the moon. Who showed more courage — Columbus in 1492 or the astronauts in 1969? Why do you think so? _____

_____

_____

_____

Which of those two events do you think was more important? Give some reasons for your choice. _____

_____

_____

_____

Many cities and places in North America and South America are named for Columbus. Can you think of some? If not, look at the index of an atlas. If there is no atlas in your classroom, the librarian can help you find one in the library.

Read the poem "Columbus" by Joaquin Miller. Your teacher or the librarian can help you find it.

D.

E.

In the West Indies, the Spaniards grew sugar, cotton, and tobacco on large plantations. They bought African slaves to work in the fields.

These drawings show how the traders packed their ships with slaves. There was barely room to lie down for the fifty-day trip to America.

Getting Ready for Chapter Four

4

Here are five vocabulary words that are used to tell about the beginning of slavery in America. Study these definitions so you will know what each word means when you see it in your reading.

prosperous   (PROS-pur-us)   Successful, rich, doing well.

citizen   (SIT-uh-zun)   A person who belongs to a country, obeys its laws, and is protected by them.

plantation   (plan-TAY-shun)   A large farm having many workers.

brand   (BRAND)   To burn a mark on something to show who owns it.

revenge   (ree-VENJ)   Doing harm to get even with someone. Getting back at a person for something he or she did.

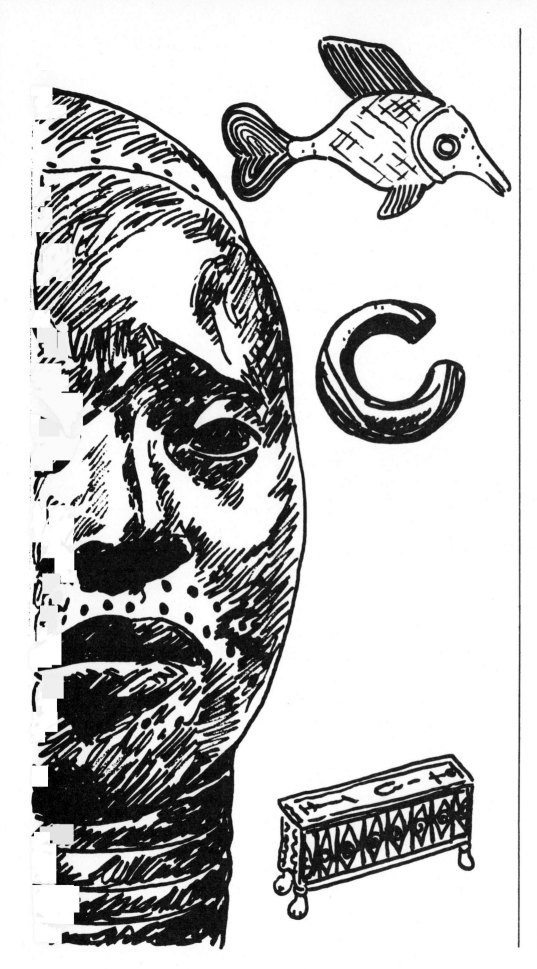

African artists made beautiful carvings and golden jewelry.

The Story of Slavery

Columbus's arrival in America was not good news for
Native Americans. It turned out to be bad news for millions
of people in Africa, too.
What was Africa like four hundred years ago?
Why did the Spanish want to have African slaves?

Black Africans came to America with the whites from Europe.
Columbus may have had some Black sailors on his ships. At any rate,
we know that Blacks were in the New World soon after 1492. Here is
how that came about.

Northern Africa is very close to Spain and *Portugal*. North Africans
and Europeans traded together for centuries. Then, about 1400, Portugal began to explore the other parts of Africa.

POR-chuh-gul

The explorers were surprised at what they saw. Africa was highly
civilized. There were powerful countries, such as *Ghana*, Mali, and
Songhay. These lands contained cities, towns, and **prosperous** farms.
The larger cities had libraries, schools, and colleges. African artists
were among the world's best.

GAH-nuh
son-GY

Dazzled by the wealth of the African cities, the *Portuguese* attacked
them. Many cities were destroyed. But something else happened that
was even worse for the Africans. The Portuguese were able to buy them
as slaves.

POR-chuh-geez

African rulers were fighting wars with each other. When they won a
battle, they took prisoners. These rulers were willing to trade their
prisoners to the Portuguese for guns and gunpowder. The Portuguese
then shipped the prisoners to Portugal, where they were sold as slaves. ●

These first slaves were homesick and frightened. After working a few
years, they were given freedom. Many of them stayed in Portugal.
They and their children became Portuguese **citizens**.

Slaves were high-priced. Only the rich could afford them. Not many
people wanted to buy slaves — at first. But after Columbus arrived in
America, all this changed. The lives of millions of Africans changed
with it.

Spanish settlers followed Columbus to the New World. They started
plantations in Latin America. Sugar, cotton, and tobacco were grown
on these large farms. Many people were needed to work in the fields.

At first, the Spaniards forced the Native Americans to do the work.
But they were not used to this kind of labor. Many were worked to
death. Others ran away. Who would take the place of these workers?

The rulers of Europe and Africa found the answer. Africans would be sent to the New World. Black slaves started arriving in large numbers in Latin America in 1517. •

Slave-trading became a business. European ships lined up off the African coast. From all over Africa, chained-up slaves were marched to trading centers. They were **branded** with their owner's mark, like cattle. When all was ready, the slaves were marched onto the ships. Up the ladders they went, men, women, and young people. Whips snapped behind them to keep them moving.

Inside a ship, the slaves were packed together tightly. They could hardly move or breathe. Many died during the trip and were thrown overboard to waiting sharks.

With luck, the trip to America lasted fifty days. Most slave ships landed first in the islands called the West Indies. These were the islands Columbus had found. Here the slaves were put to work on island plantations or sent to other parts of the New World. For most of them, life meant no freedom, all work, and very little play. The same was true for their children and their children's children.

In the back of the slaves' minds was the wish to revolt. Or escape. Or get **revenge**. The slave owners knew this, and they were afraid. Sometimes their fears came true. There was some fighting and bloodshed. But the slave revolts were put down.

So the Blacks cleared forests, raised crops, built their masters' homes. From the very beginning, they were here helping to build Europe's colonies. They added their own art, music, folk tales, and dance to the new civilization that was growing in the New World.

Answer these to review the main ideas.   **A.**

1. How did the Portuguese get African slaves? _____

_____

_____

2. Why were slaves wanted in the New World?_____

_____

_____

3. Where did most of the slave ships land when they got to America?

_____

4. What did Black people bring with them to the New World?

_____

Circle True or False.

T F 1. Large numbers of Blacks started coming to the New World in 1517.

T F 2. The Portuguese attacked African cities and destroyed them.

T F 3. Native Americans enjoyed working on the Spanish plantations.

T F 4. Slaves were well treated on the ships that brought them to America.

T F 5. Until Columbus came to America, not many people wished to buy slaves.

T F 6. In the 1400s, Africa was a poor and backward land.

T F 7. The whites never feared that the slaves would revolt.

Circle the right answer to finish each sentence.

1. Ghana, Mali, and Songhay were

   a. African countries   b. three wise men   c. Spanish colonies

2. The first prisoners the Portuguese bought were sold in

   a. Spain   b. America   c. Portugal

3. The Spanish wanted slaves to work

   a. in factories   b. on plantations   c. on ships

4. On the trip to America, many slaves

   a. died   b. escaped   c. rebelled

5.   With luck, a slave ship would reach America in

   a. a month   b. fifty days   c. three months

Choose one of these words to fit each sentence below.

   prosperous   citizen   plantation

   brand   revenge

1. A person who is loyal to a country and has the same rights as the rest

   of the people who live there is a _____ of that country.

2. When you get _____ , you get even with someone who has hurt you.

B.

C.

D.

3. To burn a special mark on something is to _____ it.

4. A large farm that has many workers is called a _____ .

5. If a business is doing well, you could call it a _____ business.

Think about and discuss in class.

E.

Why were the Portuguese surprised to find a great civilization in Africa? _____

_____

_____

Native Americans forced to be slaves ran away from the Spanish plantations. They were successful. Blacks ran away too, but they were caught.

Can you figure out why? _____

_____

_____

_____

_____

_____

_____

Ponce de Leon looked for the Fountain of Youth in the land of Florida.

Getting Ready for Chapter Five

5

Here are three vocabulary words that are used in the story of the Spanish explorers who came after Columbus. Study these definitions so you will know what each word means when you see it in your reading.

Central America
(SEN-trul) The land that lies between Mexico and South America.

treasure
(TREZH-ur) A large amount of wealth or riches, such as jewels or money.

desert
(duh-ZERT) To run away from duty. This word is spelled the same as a "desert" full of sand and cactus. You have to look at the whole sentence to know which meaning is right.

Balboa found that there was a new ocean on the western side of Panama.

Magellan took five ships west to find Asia. After three years, one ship got back home. It had sailed all the way around the world.

Magellan's voyage proved that the world really was round. It showed that the Americas were two continents Europeans had known nothing about.

The Search for New Lands

What do explorers look for, and what do they find?
An explorer named Magellan tried to sail around the
world. Did he succeed?
What did he prove?

After Columbus, many Spanish explorers came to America. They hunted for **treasure** and a way to get to Asia.

Wherever they went, the explorers asked the Native Americans where to find gold. To keep the white men from becoming angry, the native people promised them anything. "Gold and great cities are just a few miles away," they said. Or, "Try the next island." And so the explorers hurried on from one place to the next. They did not *realize* that they were being fooled. The native people were simply getting rid of them.

REE-uh-lize

The Native Americans told a *Spaniard* named Ponce de Leon that there was a Fountain of Youth somewhere to the north. To drink from this fountain would make anyone young again.

SPAN-yurd

Ponce was getting old. He was eager to find the fountain. Sailing north, he landed in Florida in 1513, but he found no fountain. Instead of life, Ponce met death at the hands of the Florida natives.

Another Spaniard named *Balboa* was shipwrecked off the coast of Panama in **Central America**. The people there told him about a great ocean just across the mountains. This time, they told the truth. When Balboa climbed the mountain in 1513, he saw the Pacific Ocean. The water stretched away endlessly to the west! •

bal-BOW-uh

News of Balboa's discovery reached an explorer named Ferdinand *Magellan*. Magellan believed he could now solve the puzzle of where Asia was. He said that Asia must lie all the way across the Pacific Ocean. And he was right!

muh-JEL-lun

In 1519, Magellan took five ships and started west from Spain. When he reached South America, he sailed south. Down the coast Magellan went, until he almost reached the tip. There he found a strait which connected the Atlantic Ocean with the Pacific.

Magellan's men were afraid to sail in unknown waters. One ship was wrecked, and another ship **deserted**. But Magellan kept going. He went through the stormy strait and kept sailing west across the wide Pacific Ocean.

Weeks went by, and no land was seen. Food ran out. The men had to eat the rats they found on the ships. When there were no more rats, they chewed on the leather ropes that held up the ship's sails. Many sailors starved to death. But at last, some of them reached the *Philippine* Islands off the coast of Asia.

FIL-uh-peen

Brave Magellan was killed in a battle with some Philippine natives. But his men kept going. They reached Spain in 1522. Out of the 265 men who had started with Magellan, only 18 came back home. The first trip around the world had taken three years.

Magellan's voyage was very important. It proved that the world was round, not flat. It showed how large the earth was, and where the oceans and continents were.

Finally, Magellan's voyage proved that the Americas were not part of Asia, after all. They were continents set off by themselves. To their east lay the Atlantic Ocean, to their west the huge Pacific. The Americas were a whole New World to the Europeans.

A.

Answer these to review the main ideas.

1. Where did Ponce de Leon land? _____

_____

2. Where was Balboa shipwrecked? _____

_____

3. Where did Magellan say Asia was? _____

_____

4. What did Magellan's voyage prove? _____

_____

B.

Circle True or False.

T F 1. Ponce de Leon finally found the Fountain of Youth.

T F 2. The Native Americans were never able to fool the explorers.

T F 3. Magellan's sailors had plenty to eat while they crossed the Pacific Ocean.

T F 4. The first trip around the world took three years.

T F 5. Magellan's trip showed how large the world was and where the continents and oceans were.

T F 6. Magellan's trip proved that the Americas were part of Asia.

28

Circle the right answer to finish each sentence.   C.

1. The explorers who followed Columbus to America were mostly

   a. Italian   b. Spanish   c. Indian

2. The explorers asked the Native Americans where to find

   a. gold   b. food   c. oil

3. Anyone who drank from the Fountain of Youth would become

   a. old   b. rich   c. young

4. Balboa found a new

   a. island   b. country   c. ocean

5. The first trip all the way around the world was started by

   a. Magellan   b. Ponce de Leon   c. Columbus

Can you give the date?   D.

1. In what year did Balboa find the Pacific Ocean? _____

2. When did Magellan begin his voyage? _____

   When was it finished? _____

Choose one of these words to fit each sentence below.   E.

          treasure   desert   Central America

1. To run away from one's duty is to _____ .

2. A large amount of jewels and money is a _____ .

3. The land lying between Mexico and South America is called
_____ .

Think about and discuss in class.   F.

Do men who wear wigs and women who wear make-up seem like Ponce

de Leon? In what way? _____

_____

In what ways were Columbus and Magellan alike? How are their stories

different?_____

_____

_____

_____

_____

_____

Do you think we know more about the moon today than people in the 1400s knew about the planet earth? List some things that were not

known before Columbus and Magellan made their trips. _____

_____

_____

_____

The Spaniards rode into Mexico City and captured Montezuma, the Aztec king.

Getting Ready for Chapter Six

6

Here are five vocabulary words that are used in the story of Cortes. Study these definitions so you will know what each word means when you see it in your reading.

conquer   (KON-kur)   To defeat or win out over someone. To win in a battle against an enemy.

persuade   (per-SWAYD)   To get others to do what you want. To talk someone into doing something.

capital   (KAP-ih-tul)   A city that is the center of government for a nation or a state.

desperate   (DES-pur-ut)   Angry and afraid because there is no hope of winning. Ready to try anything because you are losing.

violence   (VY-uh-lents)   The use of force in a way that harms somebody or breaks something. Rioting, fighting, killing, or burning.

Spanish explorers took treasure from the Aztecs and sent it home to Spain.

The angry Atzecs did not obey their king. Instead, they chased the Spaniards out of the city.

The Spaniards Take Over Mexico

This chapter tells how a Spanish leader defeated a
powerful Latin American nation.
Who were these people?
Why did the Spaniards win?

For many years Spain had the New World all to herself. Spanish *soldiers* **conquered** rich lands there for their king. The Spaniards had two goals in mind. First, they would take the *Christian* religion TO the peoples of the New World. Second, they would take FROM the New World all the treasure they could find. •

SOLE-jurz
KRIS-chun

The soldier who conquered Mexico was Hernando *Cortes*. He sailed there in 1519 with an army of six hundred Spanish and Black troops. When the ships landed, Cortes had them *destroyed*. He thought his men would fight harder if there was no chance to turn back.

kor-TEZ

duh-STROYD

Cortes was brave and daring, but a few hundred Spaniards did not conquer Mexico all by themselves. Cortes **persuaded** many nations that the Aztecs controlled to join his side. One person who gave him important help was an Aztec princess named *Dona Marina*.

DO-nyuh
muh-REEN-uh

The Aztecs were afraid of the Spaniards. They feared the white men's loud cannons. And they had never seen a horse before. A horse and rider seemed like a terrible, tall monster chasing after them. •

News that the Spanish were coming reached the Aztecs high in the mountains. The Aztecs were the strongest nation in Mexico. Their **capital** city was built on an island in a lake. High stone buildings and temples lined the streets. There were *canals* and flower gardens everywhere. The Aztec capital, later known as Mexico City, was as beautiful as any city in the world.

kuh-NALZ

The Aztec ruler was named *Montezuma*. His crown and his robes sparkled with jewels. On his feet he wore *sandals* of gold. Proud Montezuma was every inch a king. But Montezuma worried about the Spaniards. Who were these strange white soldiers marching toward his city? Could they have come from heaven? Were they gods?

mon-tuh-ZOO-muh
SAN-dulz

Montezuma sent Cortes precious gifts of cloth and gold. He hoped the Spaniards would take the gifts and go away. But seeing the gold made the Spanish hungry for more treasure. Their march continued.

Montezuma became **desperate**. He planned a surprise *attack*. But the princess Dona Marina learned of the plan and warned Cortes in time.

uh-TAK

Finally, the Spaniards marched into Mexico City. They captured Montezuma without a fight. They ripped down the temples where human sacrifices were given to the Aztec gods.

Cortes thought the Aztecs would not fight without their king. But the angry people did attack. There was **violence** in the city. Cortes asked

Montezuma to speak to the people. Surely they would obey their ruler and stop the killing. From the top of his palace, Montezuma called out to thousands of Aztecs down in the street. "Do not attack the Spaniards! Return to your homes! The white men will leave in peace!"

But the crowd was angry. They answered their king with a shower of arrows and stones. Montezuma was hit. He fell, badly hurt. He died knowing that his people hated him for giving up to the Spaniards.

Surrounded by Aztecs, Cortes and his men fought their way out of the city. To get off the island, they ran over bridges and swam in the water. Greedy soldiers had filled their pockets with Aztec gold. Those who had taken the most gold drowned.

suh-ROUND-id

In 1521 Cortes got a new army together. This time, no amount of Aztec bravery could hold out against the Spanish guns and horsemen. The Aztecs were beaten, and Cortes became the Spanish *governor* of Mexico.

GUV-ur-nur

Answer these to review the main ideas.

A.

1. What two goals did the Spaniards have in the New World? _____

_____

_____

2. Why did the Aztecs fear the Spaniards so much? _____

_____

3. Which nation in Mexico was most powerful?_____

   What was the capital city like? _____

_____

_____

_____

4. Where did Montezuma think the Spaniards came from?_____

_____

5. What finally happened to Cortes? _____

_____

Circle True or False.

T   F   1. Cortes got many people who didn't like the Aztecs to join his side.

B.

34

T F 2. Dona Marina was a Spanish princess.

T F 3. The Aztec capital city was built on an island.

T F 4. Montezuma looked forward to having Cortes visit him.

T F 5. Montezuma told the Aztecs to attack the Spaniards.

Circle the right answer to finish each sentence.   C.

1. The Aztecs had never seen
   a. gold   b. ships   c. horses

2. The Aztecs thought that a man riding a horse was a
   a. ghost   b. monster   c. god

3. Montezuma sent Cortes
   a. gifts   b. a warning   c. human sacrifices

4. Spanish soldiers tore down the Aztecs'
   a. homes   b. temples   c. bridges

Choose one of these words to fit each sentence below.   D.

desperate   persuade   conquer   capital   violence

1. A ruler often lives in the _____ city of his or her country.

2. Using _____ or doing harm to others is not a solution
   to arguments.

3. To defeat or beat one's enemies means to _____ them.

4. To feel without hope and ready to try anything is to be

   _____.

5. Trying to talk someone into doing something is trying to

   _____ him or her.

Think about and discuss in class.

Could you use this chapter to teach some lessons about greed? Look at   E.
paragraphs 1, 7, and 12. What do they tell about greedy people?

_____

_____

_____

The rich kingdom of Peru was in South America. It was ruled by a leader called the Inca.

The Man Who Conquered Peru

One of the meanest men in history was a Spaniard named Francisco *Pizarro*. Rough and tough Pizarro could neither read nor write. He was a leader who was afraid of nothing.

pih-ZAR-row

Pizarro had been in Central America with Balboa. The people there had talked about a rich kingdom in South America. It was called Peru. Pizarro persuaded the king of Spain to send him there.

In 1532 Pizarro attacked Peru. Like Cortes, he sent just a handful of men against a whole civilized nation. Pizarro was both lucky and clever. The Inca ("king") of Peru happened to be putting down a *revolt* in his land. Pizarro offered to help him. In that way, Pizarro won the Inca's friendship.

rih-VOWLT

One day the Inca and his men came to visit Pizarro. When they arrived, a Spanish priest carrying a *Bible* and a cross came out to meet them. The priest told the Inca to become a Christian. He handed him the Bible.

BY-bul

The Inca became angry. Who in the world had the right to give him orders? In his land, he was a king AND a god. The Inca threw the Bible on the ground.

At that moment, Pizarro gave a signal. Guns and cannons boomed. The Spanish had set a trap. They killed hundreds of the Inca soldiers. But they did not kill the king. They had other plans for him.

The Inca made a *bargain* with Pizarro. He promised to fill a large hall with gold and a smaller one with silver. All this treasure would be Pizarro's. In turn, the Inca would be set free.

For months the people of Peru brought treasure to the halls. They ripped down golden doors from palaces and temples. They gathered up jewels and statues. Finally, the two rooms were full.

The Inca had kept his part of the bargain. But Pizarro would not let him go. Instead, he had the Inca killed. Then Pizarro made himself governor of Peru.

For eight years Pizarro ruled that rich country. The whole time, the Spaniards kept fighting among themselves for gold. Finally Pizarro himself was murdered. But Peru remained a Spanish colony for three hundred years.

The stories of Cortes and Pizarro are much alike. Both men were bold Spanish leaders. Both men conquered the rulers of great nations. How were they able to do it?

Montezuma and the Inca were strong kings. They believed in their own greatness. Yet something about the strangeness of the Spaniards was too much for them. The horses, the cannons, the violence, and the tricks of the white men broke their spirits. In the end, the rulers were like sleepwalkers — only it was not sleep they found, but death.

BAR-gin

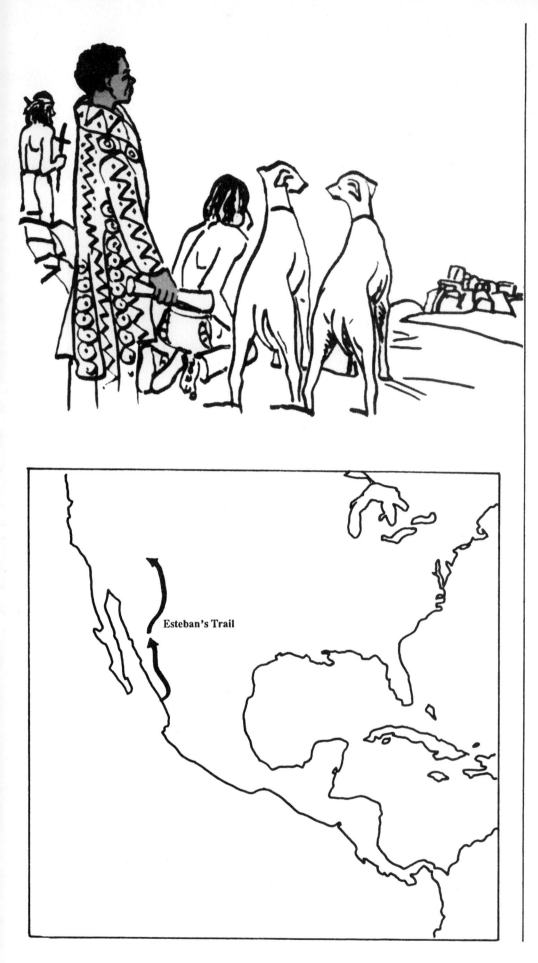

Esteban was the real leader of the expedition. He talked with the Native Americans and discovered the right trails to take.

Esteban's Trail

Esteban's trail showed other explorers how to reach California and the southwest part of the United States.

Seven golden cities were supposed to be somewhere north of Mexico. A Black slave named Esteban and a Spanish priest named Father Marcos led an expedition to look for them.

The golden cities turned out to be ordinary villages.

Getting Ready for Chapter Seven

7

Here are five vocabulary words that are used in the story of the explorer Esteban. Study these definitions so you will know what each word means when you see it in your reading.

party   (PART-ee)   A group of people sent out to do a job. A "war party" is a group of fighters. A "rescue party" goes out to save someone who is in trouble.

fearless   (FEER-les)   Afraid of nothing. Brave, daring.

suppose   (suh-POZE)   To believe something is true without knowing for sure.

ordinary   (OR-dih-nair-ee)   Not different. The same as others. Usual.

claim   (CLAYM)   To say that something belongs to you or your country because you think you or your country has a right to it.

The Fortune Hunters

This chapter is about a man who looked for gold in the southwestern part of our country.
What was unusual about him?
What did he find?

Spaniards kept hunting for gold in the New World. After conquering Mexico, they pushed north into land that is now Texas, New Mexico, and Arizona. Only Native Americans lived there then. The explorers **claimed** the land for Spain.

The first of these explorers was a Black slave named *Esteban*. He was a scout in Texas and Mexico during the 1530s. He was so good a leader that — most of the time — no one thought of him as a slave.

ES-tuh-bon

The Native Americans had never seen a Black person before. Some of them thought Esteban was a god. Everyone liked him because he was friendly and **fearless**. •

When Esteban was in Mexico, the people there told him where he could find gold. North of Mexico, they said, were seven golden cities in the land of *Cibola*. The people there were **supposed** to be very rich. They wore golden belts around their clothes. Their houses had gold roofs. Or so the stories went.

SEE-bow-luh

As always, the Spaniards were eager to find treasure. They wanted Esteban to take them to look for Cibola. But how could they let a slave be their leader? They thought awhile. Then they came up with the answer. A priest named *Friar Marcos* would be named as the leader. Esteban would go along as a guide. But Esteban would be the REAL leader. •

FRY-ur   MARK-ohs

In 1539, Esteban and Father Marcos started northward. With them were some Spaniards and Native Americans. Esteban took along two beautiful greyhound dogs.

Right from the start, Esteban was in charge. It was he who talked with Native Americans along the way and found the right trails. After awhile, Father Marcos told him to go on ahead and find Cibola. The priest and a few men would stay behind.

Father Marcos and Esteban planned to keep in touch. Esteban said he would send messengers back to the priest. The messengers would carry crosses. A small cross would mean Esteban was not finding much. A middle-sized cross would mean he was finding something important. A large cross would mean he was finding cities even larger and richer than the ones in Mexico.

After four days, Esteban sent a cross back to Friar Marcos. It was a large cross, larger than a man. Two days later he sent another large cross, with a one-word *message*. It said, "Hurry!"

MES-ij

40

Father Marcos hurried north along Esteban's trail. There were no more crosses. What had happened?

A scout who had been with Esteban brought the sad news. The Pueblo people of New Mexico had captured Esteban and questioned him. He had told them that white men were coming to their land. In fear and anger, the Pueblos had killed Esteban. Yet he had simply told them the truth. •

Later, the Spaniards sent large exploring **parties** into the western part of our country. Cibola turned out to be an **ordinary** village. Its houses were made of sand, clay, and stone — but not gold. Perhaps the sun shining on the houses had made them look golden.

Esteban is a name to remember in American history. He found no treasure, but he showed Spanish explorers the way to a new part of our country. His trail helped them find the Southwest and California. All that land was soon claimed for Spain.

A.

Answer these to review the main ideas.

1. Who was Esteban? How was he different from the Spaniards?

_____

_____

2. What did the Spaniards ask him to do?_____

_____

3. What happened to Esteban? _____

4. How did Esteban help Spain? _____

_____

B.

Circle True or False.

T F 1. White people lived in the lands that Esteban explored.

T F 2. Esteban was a slave.

T F 3. Native Americans didn't like Esteban because of his color.

T F 4. Cibola turned out to be just an ordinary village.

T F 5. Father Marcos wanted to get to Cibola ahead of Esteban.

C.

Circle the right answer to finish each sentence.

1. After conquering Mexico, Spanish explorers went north into

a. Peru   b. Texas, New   c. Florida and
                      Mexico, and   Mississippi
                      Arizona

2. Esteban kept in touch with Father Marcos by sending him

   a. letters   b. gold   c. crosses

3. The houses of Cibola were really made out of

   a. sand and clay   b. silver   c. gold

4. Esteban showed Spanish explorers the way to the American

   a. Northeast   b. Midwest   c. Southwest

Choose one of these words to fit each sentence below.

    suppose   claim   ordinary   fearless   party

1. A _____ person is not afraid of anything.

2. When something is probably true, but you don't know for sure, you

   might say, "I _____ so."

3. If there is nothing odd or unusual about your dog, you might call

   it an _____ pooch.

4. A _____ of workers might be sent out to fix up the
roads.

5. If nobody else owns a piece of land, you might be able to

   _____ it for yourself.

Think about and discuss in class.

How do you suppose the story about golden cities got started? _____

_____

Why do you think the Pueblo people killed Esteban?_____

_____

_____

How could Spanish explorers claim land for Spain when Native

Americans already lived there? _____

_____

_____

D.

E.

A Review Test on Chapters 1–7

Here are ten vocabulary words you have learned while reading the first seven chapters of this book. Choose one word to fit each sentence below.

continents	civilization	citizen	strait
ancient	capital	Latin America	council
violence	conquer		

1. A channel of water that connects the Atlantic Ocean with the Pacific Ocean could be called a _____ .

2. The lands south of the United States where the people speak mostly Spanish or Portuguese are known as _____ .

3. To defeat or crush a country means to _____ it.

4. Killing, rioting, and destroying property are forms of _____ .

5. A person who belongs to a country is a _____ of that country.

6. Something very, very old is called _____ .

7. A group of people who meet together to give advice or make rules is called a _____ .

8. The world's largest pieces of land are called _____ .

9. A city where a state or nation's government is located is the _____ city.

10. People have a _____ if they work together and have cities, laws, science, and art.

Circle the right answer to finish each sentence.

1. Scientists can tell how long ago an animal lived by testing its

   a. bones   b. tracks   c. fur

2. Women could speak out in the council meetings of the

   a. Incas   b. Pueblos   c. Iroquois

3. The Native Americans never made use of

   a. arrows   b. wheels   c. spears

4. Christopher Columbus came to America in

   a. 1492   b. 1550   c. 1513

5. Columbus thought he could get to Asia by sailing

   a. east   b. north   c. west

6. Europeans went to Asia to get

   a. jewels and spices   b. slaves   c. oil

7. Ghana, Mali, and Songhay were

   a. Italian explorers   b. Mexican nations   c. African countries

8. Magellan's expedition sailed

   a. to Mexico   b. around the world   c. to Panama

9. Columbus thought he had found

   a. America   b. Africa   c. Asia

III. Find the definition or description that matches each word or date, and write the letter on the line.

——— Peru	a.	Killed in the Philippines
——— 1492	b.	Ruler of the Aztecs
——— Cortes	c.	Conqueror of Peru
——— Artifact	d.	Land of the Incas
——— West Indies	e.	Made by human hands long ago
——— Esteban	f.	Killed searching for Cibola
——— Magellan	g.	When Columbus arrived in America
——— Montezuma	h.	Conqueror of Mexico
——— Francisco Pizarro	i.	Where most slave ships landed

IV. In your own words, write about three Native American nations that interest you. Tell where they lived and what they did. (Look back through the first seven chapters of this book to help your memory.)

44

DeSoto located the Mississippi River in 1541.

Getting Ready for Chapter Eight

8

Here are four vocabulary words that are used in the story of Spain's colonies and of the non-Spanish explorers who landed in other parts of America. Study these definitions so you will know what each word means when you see it in your reading.

jealous   (JEL-us)   Wanting what someone else has. Disliking someone because he or she is doing so well.

expedition   (eks-puh-DISH-un)   An exploring trip by a group of people.

minister   (MIN-us-ter)   An important official in a government.

strictly   (STRIKT-lee)   Going by the rules. Keeping things under tight control.

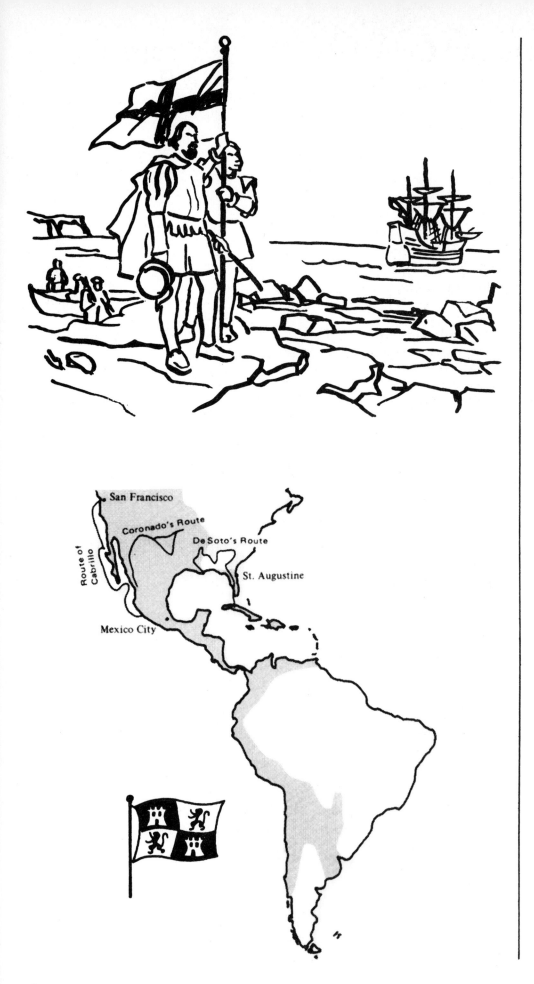

English and French explorers sailed north. In 1497, John Cabot landed in Canada. But no French or English colonies were started until many years later.

New Spain included colonies in Cailfornia, Florida, Mexico, Central America, and South America.

Other Explorers and Colonists

The Spaniards named their colonies New Spain. What was it like to live there?
Which other European countries sent explorers to America?
What lands did they find?

Spain continued to explore North America. A Spaniard named *Coronado* followed Esteban's path. In 1541 Coronado led his men northward all the way to what is now Kansas. In that same year, another explorer named De Soto located the Mississippi River. But these **expeditions** to the north found no gold or rich cities. No Spanish colonies were started in the lands they explored.

kor-uh-NAH-doh

By sea, Spanish ships arrived in California. In 1542 Juan *Cabrillo* sailed to Drake's Bay, near San Francisco. He claimed California for Spain.

kuh-BREE-yoh

Spanish settlers in Florida started the town of St. *Augustine* in 1565. St. Augustine is the oldest city in the United States. A fort built by the Spaniards still stands there today. •

saint AW-gus-teen

The Spaniards called their American colonies New Spain. This land stretched southward from California all the way down to Peru — more than three thousand miles. The colonists brought their own ways of doing things to New Spain.

The Spaniards did not rule themselves, and they did not allow others freedom. The king and his **ministers** told the people what to do. New Spain was ruled as **strictly** as old Spain. Native Americans and slaves were treated badly.

Spanish priests went among the Native Americans, spreading the Christian religion. Soldiers tore down the temples where humans were used as sacrifices to gods.

Schools were started. Native Americans learned to speak Spanish even though they had their own languages. Some learned to read Spanish books.

There were no horses in America until some were brought over from Spain. Native Americans found horses very useful for hunting. Later they used them in battles against the white men who were taking away their lands. •

When Spain found wealth in the New World, other countries in Europe became **jealous** of her. They, too, wanted to become rich. Soon they were sending their own explorers to America.

Portugal had many ships and sailors. The Portuguese landed in *Brazil* in 1500. Brazil, which is in South America, became a Portuguese colony.

bruh-ZIL

England and France sent expeditions far north of where Columbus had landed. John Cabot, sailing for England, touched the coast of Canada in 1497. The Frenchman *Cartier* explored another part of Canada in 1534. Just like Columbus, both Cabot and Cartier were looking for gold and for a way to get to Asia. England and France claimed the lands they had found, but they started no colonies until many years later.

Until the 1600s, Spain and Portugal were the only nations with colonies in North and South America. Many Native American nations still lived on land that is now the United States and Canada.

kart-YAY

Answer these to review the main ideas.

A.

1. What did Coronado and De Soto find? _____

_____

2. Who sailed to California? _____

3. Who started the oldest city in the United States?_____

_____

What is the name of that city? _____

4. Where was New Spain? _____

_____

What lands that you have read about were part of New Spain?_____

_____

What did the Spaniards think about freedom? _____

_____

5. What other countries besides Spain sent explorers to the New

World? _____

_____

Who were John Cabot and Cartier? _____

_____

What part of America did they explore?_____

_____

Circle True or False.

T F 1. Brazil was once a colony of Spain.

T F 2. De Soto and Coronado did not find any gold or rich cities.

T F 3. San Francisco is the oldest city in the United States.

T F 4. Native Americans and slaves in New Spain were badly treated.

T F 5. There were no horses in the New World before the Spaniards arrived.

T F 6. Cabot and Cartier started colonies for England and France.

Here are some dates. Tell what happened in each of these years. (Clues are given in parentheses.)

1497: _____ (English)

1534: _____ (French)

1541: _____ (Spanish)

_____ (Spanish)

1542: _____ (Spanish)

1565: _____ (Spanish)

Choose one of these words to fit each sentence below.

minister   jealous   strictly   expedition

1. People sometimes feel _____ of somebody who has things they wish they had.

2. A group of people who go on an exploring trip are members of an _____ .

3. A _____ has an important job in a government.

4. A teacher who makes students obey all the rules is one who runs a classroom _____ .

Think about and discuss in class.

Why didn't Spain start colonies in the lands that Coronado and De Soto explored? _____

_____

Why did the Spanish soldiers tear down the temples in New Spain?

_____

_____

_____

The Spaniards brought their language to the New World. There are many Spanish words that we Americans use today. *Chocolate* and *canyon* are examples. Can you think of others?_____

_____

Can you think of some cities and places that have Spanish names?

_____

_____

_____

Queen Elizabeth I ruled England in the 1500s.

John Smith wrote that one time he was caught by Native Americans and almost killed.

The treasure Spain found in America made England jealous. So English "Sea Dogs" attacked Spanish ships and stole their gold.

Getting Ready for Chapter Nine

9

Here are five vocabulary words used in the story of England's first colonies. Study these definitions so you will know what each word means when you see it in your reading.

pirate   (PY-rut) A robber who attacks ships at sea.

challenge (CHAL-unj) A dare. Words or actions that make someone fight or try to win a contest.

merchant   (MUR-chunt) One who has a business. A store owner or a trader.

permanent (PUR-muh-nent) Lasting a long time. Not wearing out or coming to an end.

democracy (duh-MOK-ruh-see) Government run by the people. Government in which the people vote for the leaders they want and vote against the ones they don't want.

John Smith made the Jamestown settlers build houses and plant crops. Jamestown became the first permanent English colony in America.

John Smith was able to make friends with the Native Americans. He helped keep the Jamestown colony from dying out.

The English Come to America

Where did England start her own American colonies?
Which colony was "lost"?
Which colony was kept alive by John Smith?

England became a strong nation in the 1500s. The country was well ruled by Queen Elizabeth I. The Queen loved her people, and the people loved her. Elizabeth was jealous of Spain and its rich colonies. She told her navy to raid the Spanish colonies and take all the treasure they could find.

The English people called these bold raiders "Sea Dogs." But the Spaniards called them **pirates** because they attacked Spanish ships and robbed them of their gold. Sir Francis Drake was the most famous English Sea Dog. Drake stole so much Spanish treasure that Queen Elizabeth made him a knight!

Next, the English started colonies of their own along the coast north of Florida. They named this land Virginia. The English hoped to find fish, lumber, and furs there. They also wanted to catch up with Spain in the New World. The first English settlement was made in 1585 at *Roanoke* Island, North Carolina. ●

ROW-uh-noke

The king of Spain tried to put a stop to the English **challenge**. In 1588, he sent a large fleet called the *Armada* to conquer England. Thousands of Spanish soldiers were on the ships.

ar-MAH-duh

To Spain's surprise, the proud Armada was badly beaten. The English ships were smaller, but much faster. They darted in and out, setting the Spanish ships on fire. The Armada was destroyed. From then on, the English navy ruled the seas.

During the war with Spain, the English had not been able to visit Roanoke. When ships finally came to bring supplies for the colonists, the colony was gone. No one was there. To this day, no one knows what happened to the one hundred settlers of the "Lost Colony." ●

Soon the English tried again to settle in America. In 1607 some **merchants** sent colonists to Virginia. The colonists were to hunt for gold and anything else of value. A share of what they found was to be given to the English merchants. Also, they were to look for any river or strait that might be a route to Asia.

The settlers landed north of Roanoke and sailed up a river. They started a colony at a place they named Jamestown, in *honor* of King James I.

ON-ur

Many of the colonists were lazy. They were not used to hard work. Some came from rich families. They spent all their time hunting for gold instead of building homes and trying to grow food. Soon they became ill and hungry.

Luckily, one of their members was a strong leader. He was a soldier named John Smith. Smith told the men they must work, or else they would starve. He made them plant crops and chop down trees for houses.

Many colonists suffered and died. Out of 105 who had landed, only 38 were alive after seven months. But Jamestown did not die out. It was the first **permanent** English colony in America.

Smith wrote about his adventures. One of his books tells how he was caught and almost killed by Native Americans. The king, *Powhatan*, ordered his men to beat Smith to death with heavy clubs. Before they could do so, the king's young daughter *Pocahontas* threw herself upon Smith to protect him. She begged her father to let Smith go. Later, Pocahontas helped Smith and the Native Americans to become friends.

pow-uh-TON

pow-kuh-HON-tus

The English had more freedom than the Spaniards did. Kings of England had to share their power with a council chosen by some of the people. The colonists had a government based on these English ideas. In 1619, their own council met for the first time in Jamestown. Freedom and **democracy** began to grow in the New World. Sad to say, in the same year, the first slaves were brought into Virginia.

Answer these to review the main ideas.

A.

1. This story tells about an English Queen. What was her name? _____

_____

What was one reason the English wanted colonies in the New

World? _____

_____

_____

2. Where did the English start their colonies? _____

_____

What did the first colonists hope to find? _____

_____

What happened to the people of Roanoke? _____

_____

3. What was the name of the first permanent English colony? _____

_____

Who was John Smith? How did he help to keep Jamestown from dying out? _____

_____

_____

4. In what way were the English different from the Spaniards? _____

_____

What kind of government was set up in Virginia? _____

_____

_____

Circle True or False.

T F 1. The first English settlements were made in Canada.

T F 2. The Spanish Armada killed all the Roanoke settlers.

T F 3. English merchants sent colonists to Virginia.

T F 4. At first, the Jamestown colonists worked hard.

T F 5. John Smith was a famous "Sea Dog."

T F 6. More than half of the Jamestown colonists died.

T F 7. The English colonists had no say in their government.

Choose one of these words to fit each sentence below.

permanent   merchant   democracy

pirate   challenge

1. A sea-going robber who steals treasure from ships is a

_____ .

2. Something that is _____ lasts a very long time.

3. A dare, or some action that makes a person try to win a contest, is

called a _____ .

4. We say there is _____ when the people of a country can choose their own leaders.

5. A storekeeper or trader who buys and sells goods is known as

a _____ .

Think about and discuss in class.

What do you think happened to the Roanoke colony? _____

_____

If you were planning to start a colony in a new land, what would you need to take along? What plans would you have to make? _____

_____

_____

_____

Was Pocahontas a real person? See what you can find out about her. Try looking in an encyclopedia or finding a book about her in the library.

_____

_____

_____

_____

D.

In November 1620, the Pilgrims landed on the coast of Massachusetts.

Getting Ready for Chapter Ten

10

Here are five vocabulary words that are used in the story of the Pilgrims. Study these definitions so you will know what each word means when you see it in your reading.

formal   (FOR-mul)   Dressed up, fancy. Done according to special rules.

worship   (WUR-ship)   To love deeply. To honor.

pilgrim   (PIL-grum)   A person who goes to distant lands to visit holy places or to show love for God.

compact   (KOM-pakt)   An agreement or treaty, usually put in writing.

equal   (EE-kwul)   The same as something else — not bigger or smaller, not better or worse.

The Pilgrims wrote out a plan for their new government.

About one hundred Pilgrims started the tiny colony at Plymouth. During the first winter in America, almost half the settlers died.

When life got better for them, the Pilgrims held a feast to give thanks.

58

The Pilgrims

Why did the Pilgrims come to America?
What was the name of the ship they sailed on?
Where did they start their colony?
Was it a success?

King James of England was stubborn and strict. He was the head of the Church of England, which was run by the English government. King James said that everyone in England must belong to his church. Those who did not would be punished.

A small group of people did not like the Church of England. They thought the service was too fancy and **formal**. They wanted to **worship** God simply, in their own way. They held secret church services in their homes. When King James heard about their meetings, he gave orders to have the people *arrested*.

uh-REST-id

The little band of worshipers escaped from England, though. They went to Holland, where they could worship as they pleased. But these English men and women were not happy in a strange, *foreign* country. They decided to go to America and live by themselves.

FOR-in

The little group talked to some English merchants. A bargain was made. The merchants would pay for a ship named the *Mayflower* to take the group to America. When they arrived, the settlers would send back furs and fish until they had paid off the costs of the trip. •

Late in the summer of 1620, about one hundred colonists sailed. Only forty of them came from the group that had lived in Holland. They were called **Pilgrims** because they were going to a far land for the sake of religion. The others were Englishmen who hoped to get rich in the New World. Today, though, when we say "the Pilgrims," we mean all of the people who sailed on the *Mayflower*.

Men, women, and children made the long, hard trip across the Atlantic Ocean. The *Mayflower* was battered by storms and lost its way. Finally, in November, 1620, the ship landed on the coast of *Massachusetts*.

mas-uh-CHOO-sits

Before the Pilgrims went ashore, they decided what kind of government they would have. They wrote out a plan for themselves. It was called the Mayflower **Compact**. The plan gave **equal** rights to all the Pilgrim men (but not the women). It was signed by rich men, poor men, and servants. The Mayflower Compact was another step toward freedom and democracy in America.

The Pilgrims settled at a place they named *Plymouth* and began building shelters to live in. Winter was coming. No one was there to help them. William Bradford, the Pilgrims' governor, wrote about those early days. He said, "They had no friends to welcome them, no

PLIM-uth

inns, no houses or towns to go to." The *Wampanoags*, a part of the *Algonquin* nation, lived in the woods.

WAM-pa-NO-ags
al-GON-kwun

In that first winter of 1620-21, half the Pilgrims died of cold and sickness. But the colonists did not give up and return to England. Miles Standish, who was a soldier, trained the men to fight. A fort with cannons was built to protect the tiny village. •

In the spring, life became much better. There was warm sunshine. The Wampanoags who lived nearby appeared and showed the Pilgrims how to plant corn. The men shot turkeys and caught fish. Plymouth's time of trouble was over. The settlement became England's second permanent colony, and that part of America became known as New England.

In the fall of 1621, the Pilgrims held a feast to give thanks for their good fortune. They invited the Wampanoags who had helped them. Ninety Wampanoags came, bringing five deer they had killed. The Pilgrims and Wampanoags ate deer, roast duck, roast goose, clams, and bread. Dessert was wild plums and berries. Young Wampanoags and Pilgrims ran races and played games together. Captain Miles Standish's little army held a parade. The *celebration* lasted three days. This was the first Thanksgiving Day in America.

sel-uh-BRAY-shun

Answer these to review the main ideas.

A.

1. Why did the Pilgrims leave England?_____

_____

2. How did the Pilgrims pay for their trip to America?_____

_____

3. Where did the *Mayflower* finally land? _____

4. How many Pilgrims died during their first winter in America? _____

_____

5. Why did the Pilgrims hold a feast in the fall of 1621? _____

_____

6. Who was Miles Standish? What did he do? _____

_____

Circle True or False.

B.

T   F   1. The *Mayflower* reached Massachusetts in November, 1620.

T F 2. Before they left the ship, the Pilgrims planned the kind of government they would have.

T F 3. As soon as the Pilgrims landed, they began to get help from the Wampanoags.

T F 4. The Pilgrims' settlement at Plymouth became the second permanent English colony in America.

T F 5. About ninety Wampanoags came to the Pilgrims' Thanksgiving feast.

C. **Circle the right answer to finish each sentence.**

1. The Church of England was a church run by the

   a. Pilgrims   b. government   c. merchants

2. The Pilgrims escaped first to

   a. America   b. Spain   c. Holland

3. The number of people who sailed on the *Mayflower* was about

   a. fifty   b. one hundred   c. two hundred

4. The Mayflower Compact was a plan for

   a. a government   b. a ship   c. a fort

5. The Pilgrims agreed to give equal rights to

   a. all men   b. men and women   c. men, women, and children

6. The Pilgrims named their settlement

   a. Plymouth   b. Boston   c. Massachusetts

7. Neighboring Wampanoags showed the Pilgrims how to

   a. plant corn   b. shoot cannons   c. build houses

D. **Choose one of these words to fit each sentence below.**

   compact   formal   equal

   pilgrim   worship

1. For weddings and other _____ times in our lives, there are rules telling us how to dress and what to say and do.

2. If you show very great love for a person, you might say that you _____ him or her.

61

3. People making a long trip to visit a holy place or to show love for God are known as _____s.

4. When two people make a bargain or an agreement, they might write it all down and call it a _____ .

5. Things that are the same size are _____.

Think about and discuss in class.

E.

Would you have enjoyed eating the food the Pilgrims served at the first Thanksgiving feast? What things would you have missed? _____

_____

What might have happened if the Pilgrims had not made up the Mayflower Compact as a plan for governing themselves? _____

_____

_____

_____

What do you know about the first settlers in the state where you live? Did they have troubles like the Pilgrims? _____

_____

_____

This chapter gives an unusual meaning for "compact." What other meanings does this word have?_____

_____

_____

Roger Williams was a church leader who spoke up for freedom of religion.

Getting Ready for Chapter Eleven

Here are four vocabulary words that are used in the story of the thirteen English colonies. Study these definitions so you will know what each word means when you see it in your reading.

found   (FOUND)   To start or begin something, such as a city, a colony, or a business.

expensive   (eks-PEN-siv)   High-priced, costly.

popular   (POP-yoo-lur)   Well liked. Well thought of by many people.

toleration   (tol-ur-AY-shun)   Allowing people to think or do as they please, even if you don't agree with their ideas.

William Penn hoped people of all religions would come and enjoy freedom in Pennsylvania. He had signs put up in Europe's cities to advertise his colony.

William Penn was very rich, but he believed in treating all people as equals.

Colonists from Holland settled along the Hudson River in New York.

The Thirteen Colonies

This chapter tells about seven of the thirteen colonies.
Each one has an interesting history.
Why did two Puritans leave Massachusetts to start new
colonies in Rhode Island and Connecticut?
Which colony was started by the Dutch?
Which colony was started to help poor people?
Where did Roman Catholics settle?
Who was William Penn?

After the Pilgrims, many other settlers came to Massachusetts. In 1630 a thousand English colonists settled around Boston. These people were called *Puritans* because they wanted to make the Church of England "pure." Over the next ten years, twenty thousand Puritans came to live in Massachusetts. The king and the Church of England were glad to see them go.

PYOOR-uh-tunz

The Massachusetts Puritans were very strict about religion. They had come to America to worship in their own way. When people of other faiths came to the colony, they were not welcome. The Puritans ordered them to leave. A few who kept coming back were killed.

Two church leaders in Massachusetts disagreed with the Puritans. These leaders were Thomas Hooker and Roger Williams. Both said people should be free to worship and think as they pleased. Thomas Hooker left Massachusetts with his followers in 1636. Hooker started the colony of *Connecticut*. Roger Williams was forced to leave by the Puritans. If he had stayed in Massachusetts, he would have been put in jail. So Williams bought land from the *Narragansetts* and **founded** the colony of *Rhode Island* in 1636. •

kuh-NET-uh-kut

nar-a-GAN-suts
rode I-lund

New York was founded by the Dutch, the people of Holland. The Dutch settled along the Hudson River. They traded goods to the native people for beaver furs. These furs were valuable. They could be sold in Europe to make **expensive** clothing for the rich.

The Dutch founded New York City in 1626. They paid the Native Americans there only twenty-four dollars for the land. Forty years later, the English took over the whole New York colony from the Dutch. •

William Penn started the colony of *Pennsylvania* in 1681. Penn was an Englishman who belonged to a religious group called Friends, or Quakers. The Friends believed that all people were equal. They hated war and would not take part in it.

pen-sul-VAYN-yuh

William Penn was very rich. Yet he treated everyone as an equal, including the Native Americans. When he came to Pennsylvania, he paid them for the land. He also promised he would never go to war with them.

Penn welcomed everyone to his colony. He *advertised* all over Europe, telling people to come to Pennsylvania and enjoy freedom. Quakers, Catholics, *Protestants*, and Jews from many countries answered his call. They lived together in peace and worked hard at their jobs. Pennsylvania became the richest colony in North America. ●

AD-vur-tyzd

PROT-us-tunts

Like the Pilgrims and Puritans, Roman Catholics were not **popular** in England. Many Catholics lost their rights and *property*.

PROP-ur-tee

Lord Baltimore was one Roman Catholic whom the king still liked. Baltimore asked the king for some land in America where Catholics could live safely. The king agreed, and Baltimore started a colony named Maryland. This was in honor of England's Queen Mary.

In 1634 the first ships arrived in Maryland. Both Catholic and Protestant colonists settled there. They treated the Native Americans fairly and did not suffer from war or hunger.

The Maryland colony grew. After a few years, there were many more Protestants than Catholics. The Catholics were afraid that they would lose their property and the right to vote.

In 1649, Catholics and Protestants reached an agreement. The government of Maryland passed the **Toleration** Act. This law said that all Christians in the colony could worship in any way they wished. The Toleration Act gave Roman Catholics the freedom and protection they needed. ●

Georgia was the last colony to be settled. It was the farthest south of all the thirteen colonies. Georgia's next-door neighbor, Florida, was still owned by Spain.

James *Oglethorpe* founded Georgia in 1733. Oglethorpe had two reasons for starting the colony. First, he wanted Georgia to be English land. He wanted a colony that could fight off any Spanish attacks from Florida. Second, Oglethorpe wanted to help Englishmen who were poor and out of work. In Georgia, they could get a new start in life and a chance to enjoy freedom.

OW-gul-thorp

This chapter has told about seven of England's thirteen colonies in North America. The other six colonies were New Hampshire, New Jersey, Delaware, Virginia, North Carolina, and South Carolina.

Answer these to review the main ideas.

A.

1. Who came to Massachusetts in 1630? Why did they come? _____

_____

2. Who were Thomas Hooker and Roger Williams? _____

_____

3. What colony was settled by the Dutch? _____

   Who took that colony away from them? _____

4. What was William Penn's religion? _____

   How did Penn treat other people? _____

5. How did the Toleration Act help Roman Catholics in Maryland?

   _____

   _____

6. Why did James Oglethorpe found Georgia? _____

   _____

   _____

B.

Tell the date for each of these.

1. The Puritans came to America: _____

2. Thomas Hooker founded Connecticut: _____

3. Roger Williams founded Rhode Island: _____

4. William Penn started the colony of Pennsylvania: _____

5. The Toleration Act was passed: _____

6. Georgia was founded: _____

C.

Circle the right answer to finish each sentence.

1. The Puritans settled near

   a. Boston   b. New York City   c. Baltimore

2. A colony founded by people who left Massachusetts was

   a. New Jersey   b. Georgia   c. Connecticut

3. A colony where Roman Catholics could live safely was started by

   a. Roger Williams   b. Thomas Hooker   c. Lord Baltimore

4. James Oglethorpe wanted to help England's

   a. poor people   b. traders   c. old people

5. Quakers, Jews, Catholics, and Protestants from many countries
   were welcomed to the colony of

   a. Massachusetts   b. Pennsylvania   c. Maryland

Choose one of these words to fit each sentence below.

found   expensive   popular   toleration

1. Something that is _____ costs a lot of money to buy.

2. Many people think that the Puritans should have showed more

   _____ for people they disagreed with.

3. A _____ song is one that is liked by lots of people.

4. A rich person might give money to _____ a new school,
   a library, or a hospital.

A Map of the Thirteen Colonies.

Six names are filled in. Write in the names of the other seven colonies, using the clues that are given for each letter.

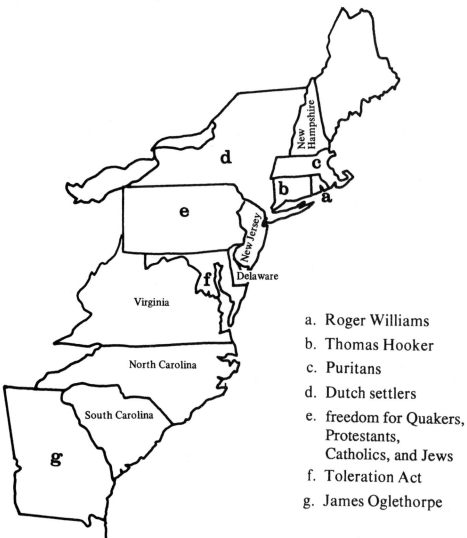

a. Roger Williams

b. Thomas Hooker

c. Puritans

d. Dutch settlers

e. freedom for Quakers,
   Protestants,
   Catholics, and Jews

f. Toleration Act

g. James Oglethorpe

Where are the states of Vermont and Maine? They were not separate colonies. Vermont was part of New York and was also claimed by New Hampshire. Maine was part of the Massachusetts colony.

D.

E.

Life in the Colonies

It took hard work to build thirteen colonies in the American wilderness. Trees had to be cut down so that the land could be turned into fields for farming. Homes, churches, and stores had to be built. There was no *machinery* like we have today. People had to work with their hands, using simple tools.

muh-SHEEN-ree

The New England colonists soon discovered that their soil was thin and rocky. It was not good for farming. Many people turned to other ways of making a living. They built ships from lumber taken from the forests. These ships carried fish and lumber to seaports all over the world. They also carried slaves from Africa to the West Indies.

New Englanders believed strongly in religion and education. Children were taught to read, so that they could study the Bible. Ministers had to go to college to learn how to preach. Harvard is America's oldest college. It was founded in 1636 at *Cambridge*, Massachusetts. ●

KAME-brij

South of New England lay the Middle Colonies. They included New York, New Jersey, Pennsylvania, and Delaware. The soil in these colonies was rich and good for growing wheat. Since wheat is made into bread, the Middle Colonies were called the "bread colonies." The leading cities were New York and Philadelphia.

One of America's leading citizens in the 1700s was Benjamin Franklin of Philadelphia. Franklin was known all over the world as a thinker, writer, and inventor. Franklin once flew a kite in a thunderstorm to catch lightning and prove that it was a kind of electricity. It was a dangerous *experiment*. He invented a new kind of stove, better eyeglasses, chemical *fertilizer* for soil and many other useful things. He

ek-SPEHR-uh-munt
FUR-tuh-lyz-ur

also served the government of his city and his colony. Before the Revolution, the colonists sent Franklin to speak for them in England. During the war he was a member of Congress, and he helped persuade the French to join the American side. With his brilliant mind, Benjamin Franklin helped the Middle Colonies to become strong and free.

The Southern Colonies included Maryland, Virginia, the Carolinas, and Georgia. Good soil and a mild *climate* meant good farming. Cotton, tobacco, and rice were grown.

KLY-mut

Rich farmers called planters owned large pieces of land called plantations. The work on these plantations was done by slaves who had been brought to America against their will. Some planters were kinder to their slaves than others. But none of them treated the Blacks as equals. Slaves were thought to be property, not people. They had no rights and were given no education.

There were also many small farms in the South. These were often run by the Scotch-Irish from Ireland. The small farmers had no use for either planters or slaves. They lived near the wilderness and were good hunters and soldiers.

Today, newspapers tell us what the government is doing. In colonial times, newsmen could only write good things about the government. If they wrote bad things, they could be punished.

Getting Ready for Chapter Twelve

12

Here are five vocabulary words used in the story of a court case that helped make American newspapers free from government control. Study these definitions so you will know what each word means when you see it in your reading.

criticize   (KRIT-uh-syz)   To judge the good and bad parts of something. To point out faults and weaknesses.

expose   (eks-POZE)   To find out what is wrong and tell people about it. To uncover some hidden crime or bad deeds.

furious   (FYOOR-ee-us)   Very angry.

jury   (JOOR-ee)   A group of citizens who hear the facts in a court trial and decide if a person should be punished.

principles   (PRIN-suh-pulz)   Main ideas. Rules that tell how something works — the "principles of baseball" or "principles of math."

In his printing shop, John Peter Zenger printed a newspaper called the New York Weekly Journal.

When John Peter Zenger wrote stories that criticized Governor Cosby, the governor had him arrested. But the jury decided Zenger's stories were true and set him free.

New York's judges were chosen by the governor.

Freedom of the Press

Newspapers, radios, and TV tell us what our
government is doing every day. Mayors and governors
don't always like what the newspeople say, but they cannot
throw them in jail.
This chapter tells how colonial newspapers got the
right to print the truth in their pages. This right is known
as "freedom of the press."

Americans love freedom. No one has all the freedom he or she wants, because there are laws we must obey. To get along with each other, we must have some rules. But the United States is a free country. It is a democracy. That means that the citizens choose how the government will be run. If we do not like the men and women who are running things for us, we can vote them out of office on *election* day.

ee-LEK-shun

In order to be free, we must be able to **criticize** our leaders. Of course we must not print or broadcast lies about them. But we cannot be put in jail for telling the truth. In the 1700s, people were not so free. ●

John Peter Zenger was a German who came to the American colonies with his father in 1710. His father died on the ship on the way over. Young Zenger arrived alone in New York City. He was thirteen years old.

Zenger got a job as a printer. In 1733 he started a newspaper called the New York Weekly *Journal.* "The purpose of this paper," Zenger wrote, "is to explain the **principles** of liberty and to **expose** those people who wish to destroy them."

JUR-nul

The governor of the New York colony was William Cosby. Like all colonial governors, Cosby had been picked for the job by the king of England. Cosby was a friend of the king and queen. He was also greedy. He took all the money he could get from the people of New York.

The New York Weekly Journal attacked Cosby. It said that New Yorkers would become slaves unless they were treated better by their governor. Cosby was **furious**. In 1734 he had Zenger arrested and sent to prison. Zenger was in jail for nine months.

In 1735 John Peter Zenger was tried in court for criticizing Governor Cosby. The trial was held in New York City. People in both England and America were interested in the case. Could the English punish every American newspaper writer who dared to criticize them? Would the colonists win freedom of the press? ●

Judges who owed their jobs to Governor Cosby sat at their desks in the courtroom. Under English law, these men would decide whether the stories Zenger had written were true or false. Of course the judges would side with the governor. It looked as if Zenger had no chance at all. But then came a surprise. Friends of Zenger had persuaded the best lawyer in the colonies to defend him.

Into the courtroom walked Andrew Hamilton of *Philadelphia*. He was an old man who had traveled a hundred difficult miles to help the side of freedom. Hamilton was asked if Zenger had printed stories criticizing Cosby. "Yes," said Hamilton. "He did."

fil-uh-DEL-fee-uh

The judges smiled. The case was about over. They would decide that the stories were false, and Zenger would go back to jail.

"But suppose the things Zenger said are true?" Hamilton asked.

The chief judge answered, "It is up to the judges to decide whether they are true or not."

Hamilton argued that this was not so. He said it should be up to the **jury** to decide the case. The jury was made up of ordinary citizens. They were plain men who would judge the facts fairly. If they thought that Zenger had written the truth, he should go free.

The judges finally agreed to let the jury decide. Juries were supposed to do what the judges told them to, anyway. Again, the judges were in for a surprise.

"Not *guilty!*" the jury declared. Zenger had simply printed the truth. He could not be punished for that.

GIL-tee

Zenger's victory was an important one for freedom. It gave the colonists the liberty to speak and write the truth. No longer did they have to keep silent when the king's governors cheated them.

The Zenger case was a warning to England. True, England had founded the colonies. The English flag flew over them. But the colonists demanded fair treatment from the English. If they didn't get it, there might some day be war between England and her American colonies.

Answer these to review the main ideas.

A.

1. What does "freedom of the press" mean? _____

_____

2. How did Governor Cosby treat the people of New York? _____

_____

3. Why was John Peter Zenger tried in court? _____

_____

4. Who was going to decide whether or not Zenger was guilty? _____

_____

Who did Andrew Hamilton say should judge the case? _____

_____

What happened? _____

_____

_____

5. Why was Zenger's victory important for democracy? _____

_____

Circle the right answer to finish each sentence.   **B.**

1. Colonial governors were chosen by

   a. the English king   b. the colonists   c. the newspapers

2. John Peter Zenger was tried in court for

   a. stealing money   b. printing a paper   c. criticizing
                                            Governor Cosby

3. Zenger was defended by

   a. Andrew Hamilton   b. Governor Cosby   c. his father

4. The judges thought that the case should be decided by

   a. themselves   b. the jury   c. the king

5. The Zenger trial took place in

   a. 1735   b. 1710   c. 1776

6. Under English law, Zenger could NOT be punished if the things he
   wrote were

   a. false   b. true   c. critical

Choose one of these words to fit each sentence below.   **C.**

    criticize   furious   principle

    expose   jury

1. The _____s of arithmetic tell you what rules to use to
   solve a problem.

2. A group of people chosen to decide the facts in a law case is called

   a _____ .

75

3. A person who becomes very angry is _____ .

4. When you point out someone's faults or weaknesses, you are

   _____ him or her.

5. To uncover something wrong and let everybody know about it is

   to _____ it.

D.

Think about and discuss in class.

Why did Andrew Hamilton want the Zenger case decided by the jury

instead of by the judges? _____

_____

_____

The colonial New York judges were chosen by the governor. How are
judges chosen today? Can they lose their jobs if they don't please the

government? _____

_____

_____

Does it take courage to criticize other people? Is it always wise to

criticize? What chances do we take when we criticize others? _____

_____

_____

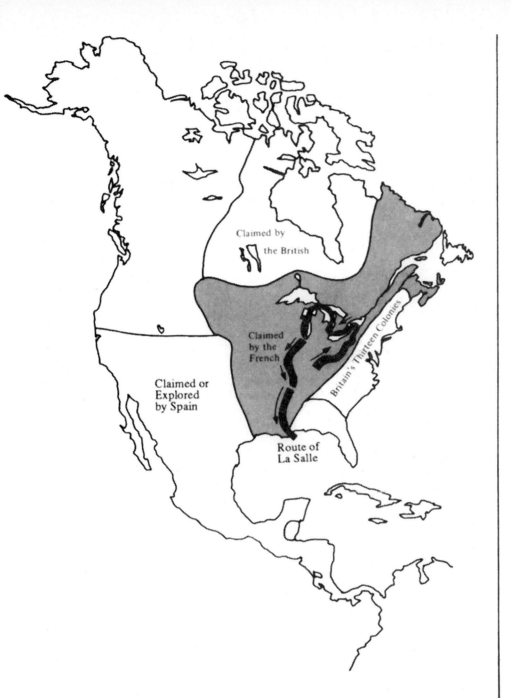

Who claimed more land in America — the British, or the French? Which country had the most colonists?

Getting Ready for Chapter Thirteen

13

Here are three vocabulary words used in the story of the French and Indian War. Study these definitions so you will know what each word means when you see it in your reading.

ally   (AL-ly)   A country that is friendly with another country and helps it in time of war.

missionary (MISH-un-air-ee) A person sent out by a church group to teach their religion in other lands.

tax   (TAKS) Money a government collects from the people to pay for running the country.

British soldiers used to march straight into battle as if they were in a parade.

From the Native Americans, the French learned how to surpirse the enemy. They hid behind trees until the British came up close. Then the French opened fire at close range.

France Challenges England — and Loses

What did France and England fight about?

How did the French and Indian War get its name?

After the English won the war, what did they do?

This chapter uses a new name for the English. England and all her colonies became known as the British Empire. People loyal to the Empire were called British.

England's American colonies were built along a narrow strip of the Atlantic Coast. Farther inland, the French were settling a much larger piece of land. In 1608 they started the colony of *Quebec* in Canada. Then they explored the Great Lakes and claimed that region.

kwuh-BEK

In 1682 a Frenchman named La Salle led an expedition down the Mississippi River. His men paddled canoes south from the Great Lakes all the way to the Gulf of Mexico. La Salle claimed the whole Mississippi River and land on both sides of it for the French. He named it *Louisiana* in honor of King Louis of France.

loo-ee-zee-AN-uh

The French did not come to North America in large groups, the way the English did. Frenchmen were not interested in clearing the land for towns and farms. Instead, they trapped animals in the forests for valuable furs. French **missionaries** went into the wilderness to teach the Christian religion to the Native Americans.

Instead of towns, the French built forts. Soldiers warned people of other nations to keep off French land. As they built more forts, the French found themselves on land that England claimed. Neither country would give in to the other. Each hoped to drive the other one out of North America. ●

The war between England and France is called the French and Indian War. The French and their Native American or Indian **allies** were on one side. England and the thirteen colonies were on the other. Fighting began in 1754 in western Pennsylvania.

At first, the French won battle after battle. The Native Americans had taught them how to fight in the wilderness. The best way was to hide behind trees and shoot at enemies when they got close.

The English did not understand this kind of war. In a battle, they headed straight toward the enemy. They marched together, as if they were in a parade. That was the way wars were fought in Europe. In their red coats, the British made perfect targets for enemy guns.

After two years, the British changed their leaders and *generals*. Men and supplies were increased greatly. Then they began to win. They captured one French fort after another. The biggest one, at Quebec, was taken in 1759. The one at *Montreal* was captured in 1760. In 1763 the

JEN-ur-ulz

mon-tree-ALL

French gave up. France had to give Canada — and nearly all her other American land — to the British. •

The British won the French and Indian War. But it was very expensive, as all wars are. When the fighting was over, Britain still had to keep a large army in America. Soldiers were needed to keep order in the lands taken from the French. They protected the settlers from angry Native Americans.

To raise money for this army, the British made the people in the colonies pay taxes. **Taxes** were placed on goods like tea and sugar. The colonists had to pay an extra penny or two every time they bought these goods. The extra money went to the British government to pay expenses.

Making the colonists pay taxes was fair, the British thought. The money was used to protect them from Native American raids. But the colonists were furious. They were not used to being taxed.

The problem of taxes caused a split between the British and their American colonies. The story of the fight is told in Chapter Fourteen.

A.

Answer these to review the main ideas.

1. What land did La Salle claim for France?_____

_____

2. What was the name of the war between England and France? _____

_____

3. What did the French learn from the Native Americans about fighting

   wars in America? _____

_____

4. Why did the British make the American colonists pay taxes?_____

_____

B.

Circle True or False.

T F 1. The French sent more colonists to America than the English did.

T F 2. Native Americans taught the French soldiers to march straight toward the enemy.

T F 3. The American colonists did not want to pay taxes to England.

T F 4. The British won the French and Indian War.

T F 5. When the war ended, all the British soldiers went home to England.

Circle the right answer to finish each sentence.

C.

1. The French were interested mainly in

   a. growing crops   b. fur-trapping   c. building cities

2. In 1682, the Frenchman LaSalle explored the

   a. Mississippi River   b. Hudson River   c. Connecticut River

3. Louisiana was named after King Louis of

   a. England   b. Spain   c. France

4. The British used the tax money to pay their

   a. governors   b. soldiers   c. missionaries

5. Colonists had to pay an extra penny or two when they

   a. bought tea   b. took trips   c. bought land

Choose one of these words to fit each sentence below.

D.

tax   missionary   ally

1. Governments get the money they need by ordering people to

   pay a _____.

2. A person who teaches his or her religion to people in other lands

   is a _____.

3. Someone who is your _____ will help you fight your

   enemies.

Think about and discuss in class.

E.

Why do you think England was stronger than France in the French and

Indian War? Which side had the most people living in America? _____

_____

No one likes to be taxed. What things is tax money used for today?

What would happen if we had no taxes? _____

_____

_____

The colonists thought a tax on tea was unfair. Instead of paying the tax, they threw the tea into Boston Harbor.

Getting Ready for Chapter Fourteen

14

Here are five vocabulary words that are used in the story of the colonists' fight against Britain. Study these definitions so you will know what each word means when you see it in your reading.

revolution	(rev-uh-LOO-shun) An uprising or revolt against the leaders of the government. A big change in government that happens when people use force to throw out their rulers.
Parliament	(PAR-luh-ment) The group of people who are chosen to make the laws for their country. A name for the law-making council of Britain.
defy	(dee-FY) To stand up to or challenge someone powerful. To go against or disobey.
representative	(rep-ree-ZENT-uh-tiv) Someone chosen by a group of people to speak out for all of them.
independent	(in-duh-PEND-ent) Free. Not ruled or controlled by someone else. Able to take care of yourself.

Congress chose George Washington to lead the American armies.

In the Revolution, five thousand Blacks helped the colonists fight the British.

Molly Pitcher carried water to the thirsty gunners. In one battle, she helped Americans load their cannons, too.

Early in the war, the Americans lost many battles. But George Washington kept his little army going. They did not give up.

The American Revolution

Why did the Americans hate to be taxed by England?
How did the American Revolution start?
Who helped the colonists in the fight?

Chapter 14

"Pay taxes to England? Not on your life!" cried the American colonists. When they were ordered to pay a tax on tea, they went wild. Climbing onto the ships that had brought the tea, the Americans threw it into Boston harbor. This was the famous "Boston Tea Party" of 1773.

The Americans were angry. Britain made them obey British laws but did not give the colonists a chance to vote on those laws. The colonists wanted to make their own laws. Or else they wanted the same rights that Englishmen had. They wanted to send **representatives** to England. The representatives would vote in the British **Parliament**. They would attack any unfair tax laws aimed at America. But the British would not let Americans be members of Parliament. They did not want to give up any of their power.

In anger, the American colonists dared to **defy** the strongest nation on earth. They trained themselves to be soldiers. They said they could grab their guns and be ready to fight the British in a single minute. They called themselves "minutemen."

In April 1775, the American **Revolution** broke out at Lexington, Massachusetts. The minutemen had hidden guns and supplies at nearby Concord. When the British went looking for them, the minutemen blocked the way. Some shots were fired, and the war was on. •

The thirteen colonies formed a government of their own, which met at Philadelphia. It was called the Continental Congress. The Congress chose George Washington of Virginia to lead the American armies. Washington had fought in the French and Indian War. He was a brave soldier and a great leader.

The Americans were fighting the best army in the world. In the beginning, they lost many battles. But they showed courage even when they were beaten. Some Americans still hoped that peace could be made with England. They felt close ties with their English friends and relatives. But by 1776, there was no chance for peace. The war had gone on too long. There was too much hurt and anger on both sides for the armies to stop fighting.

On July 4, 1776, the colonists put their feelings in writing. The United States of America declared it was free, or **independent**, from England. July 4 — Independence Day — is our nation's birthday that we celebrate every year. The Declaration of Independence was written by Thomas Jefferson of Virginia. It was signed by Benjamin Franklin,

John Adams, and many other great Americans in the Continental Congress. ●

In 1777, the American army caught the British in a trap. They surrounded them at *Saratoga*, New York. At the Battle of Saratoga, a large British army *surrendered* and became prisoners. This American victory was what the French had been waiting for.

sair-uh-TOW-guh
suh-REN-durd

France had been watching the war carefully. The French wanted to get even with their old enemy, England. After Saratoga, they were sure that they could help the Americans win. So the French sent a large army to America.

In 1781 the French and Americans caught the British in another trap. This one was at Yorktown, Virginia, on the Atlantic Coast. The British tried to escape by sea, but the French navy was waiting for them. Finally the British surrendered. ●

Many people who believed in freedom and *equality* helped the Americans in the war. Five thousand Blacks fought on the American side. No one wanted freedom more than they did.

ee-KWOL-uh-tee

Women sometimes took part in the war, too. Mrs. Mary Hays followed her soldier husband wherever he went. In one battle, she took his place firing a cannon when he was hurt. She also carried water to the other gunners, who gave her the nickname "Molly Pitcher."

There were *heroes* on both sides in the American Revolution. But one man stands out above all others. He was General George Washington. He kept on fighting when his little army was on the edge of defeat. During the hardest times, Washington knew how to strike back against the enemy. Truly he was — and is — the Father of His Country. ●

HEER-owz

The peace treaty ending the Revolution was signed in 1783. The United States of America was a free country. It stretched from the edge of Canada to the border of Florida. From east to west, it ran from the Atlantic Ocean all the way to the Mississippi River. The new United States was twice the size of the old thirteen colonies.

Hard times lay ahead for the newly born United States. Americans had done the impossible. They had beaten the British and won their independence. But the country was run down from the war. The Continental Congress and the state governments had no money. The soldiers had not been paid. It was now up to the American people to get together. Their job was to learn how to make democracy work.

Answer these to review the main ideas.

A.

1. Why were the colonists angry over being taxed by the British? What

   did Americans want? _____

_____

_____

2. When and where did the American Revolution start? _____

_____

3. When is our nation's birthday? _____

   What happened on that date? _____

_____

4. Why did the French help the Americans? _____

_____

5. Who was the greatest hero of the Revolution? _____

_____

Draw lines to match the dates with the events. **B.**

    1773 •   • American Revolution
                          begins at Lexington

    1775 •   • United States declares
                          independence at Philadelphia

    1776 •   • peace treaty signed

    1781 •   • angry colonists have
                          a Boston Tea Party

    1783 •   • Americans and French
                          beat the British at Yorktown

Circle the right answer to finish each sentence. **C.**

1. The colonists were furious when the British put a tax on

   a. eggs   b. tea   c. milk

2. The colonists who trained themselves to fight the British were called

   a. minutemen   b. representatives c. congressmen

3. The American government at Philadelphia was called

   a. the minutemen   b. the Continental c. Parliament
                           Congress

4. The Declaration of Independence was written for the Congress by

   a. Washington   b. Franklin   c. Jefferson

86

5. A country that sent an army to help the Americans was

   a. Canada   b. Spain   c. France

D.

Choose one of these words to fit each sentence below.

     revolution   representative   Parliament

     defy   independence

1. When a country overthrows its government, it goes through

   a _____ .

2. A person who is chosen to speak for a group is the group's

   _____ .

3. To stand up to and challenge someone who has power means

   to _____ him or her.

4. Freedom to run our own affairs is called _____ .

5. The lawmaking body of England is named _____ .

E.

Think about and discuss in class.

Why were Blacks eager to fight on the American side in the Revolution?

Why might some Blacks have wanted the British to win? _____

_____

_____

The Americans used violence when they threw the British tea into Boston Harbor. Other parts of this book have told about violence, too.

Give some examples from earlier chapters. _____

_____

_____

_____

Was all of that violence necessary? Could there have been other ways to do things? Choose one of the examples you listed above, and tell what

YOU would have done. _____

_____

_____

Final Review Test

Here are fifteen vocabulary words you have learned while reading this book. Choose one word to fit each sentence below.

democracy	jury	colony
artifact	criticize	revolution
desert	permanent	pilgrim
tax	representative	independence
challenge	found	expedition

1. A person chosen by a group to carry out its wishes is the group's _____ .

2. A dare to someone to try and beat us at something is a _____ .

3. Anything _____ will last a very long time.

4. An exploring trip by an organized group is called an _____ .

5. A person who travels to distant lands to visit holy places is a _____ .

6. To begin a new city or a new settlement is to _____ it.

7. When a country plants a settlement in a strange land, it has started a _____ .

8. When a country overthrows its rulers, it goes through a _____ .

9. A government run by the people themselves is called a _____ .

10. To point out the weaknesses of people or actions means that we _____them.

11. A group of people chosen to judge someone in court is called a _____ .

88

12. An object made by human hands long ago is an

   _____ .

13. To run away from one's duty is to _____ .

14. Money the government collects to pay expenses is a

   _____ .

15. Those who are free from the control and rule of others have

   _____.

Circle the right answer to finish each sentence.   II.

  1. Christopher Columbus landed in America in

  a. 1392   b. 1497   c. 1492

  2. The Spaniards called their American colonies

  a. Mexico   b. New Spain   c. North America

  3. The Portuguese started a colony in

  a. Cuba   b. Peru   c. Brazil

  4. In 1585 the English started a settlement at

  a. Plymouth,   b. Roanoke Island   c. St. Augustine,
     Massachusetts   Florida

  5. The first permanent English settlement in America was at

  a. Jamestown,   b. Roanoke Island   c. St. Augustine,
     Virginia   Florida

  6. A country that helped the colonists in the American Revolution
    was

  a. Holland   b. Canada   c. France

  7. The holiday that has come down to us from the Pilgrims is called

  a. Christmas   b. Halloween   c. Thanksgiving

Circle True or False.   III.

T   F   1. The first Americans came from Africa thousands of years
           ago.

T   F   2. There were no horses in the New World before the Spaniards
           arrived.

T F 3. In the French and Indian War, French colonists fought the Native Americans.

T F 4. The Pilgrims settled in Massachusetts at a place they called Plymouth.

T F 5. William Penn advertised all over Europe for colonists to come to Pennsylvania.

T F 6. Puritans wanted people of all religions to enjoy freedom in Massachusetts.

T F 7. France had to give up its colonies in America after the French and Indian War.

Find the definition or description that matches each word or date, and write the letter on the line.   IV.

———— Latin America   a. told the Jamestown settlers to build homes and plant crops

———— Spanish Armada   b. America's birthday

———— Juan Cabrillo   c. founded by the Dutch

———— Continental Congress d. The man for whom the Americas are named

———— John Smith   e. government run by the people

———— July 4, 1776   f. where mostly Spanish and Portuguese are now spoken

———— democracy   g. badly defeated by English navy

———— Americus Vespucius   h. founded Georgia in 1733

———— New York   i. governed America during the American Revolution

———— Oglethorpe   j. claimed California for Spain in 1542

In your own words, write about any two colonies that were started by England in America. Who founded these two colonies? In what year were they started? Tell why the colonies were started or what life was like there. You may use this book to help you.

90